Selah

A Life in Poetry

Carolyn L. Houghton

This book is a work of fiction. The characters, incidents and dialogue are drawn from the authors' imaginations and are not to be construed as real or pertaining to a real event. Any resemblance to actual events or persons, living or dead, is entirely coincidental.

Copyright © 2023 Celia Ann Buchanan Walsh Trust All rights reserved. No part of this book may be used or reproduced in any manner whatsoever without written permission except in the case of brief quotations embodied in critical articles and reviews. For information address DancingCrowsPress@gmail.com

ISBN 13: 978-1-951543-22-8

Library of Congress Control Number: 2023907425

Copy art and layout by Colin S. Wheeler, PhD MFA

Dedication

To Celia, her loving, kind, wonderful light bringer. You were and always will be the source of joy she felt every day.

To her family, Chip, Dolly, Jon, and the beautiful children and grandchildren she treasured.

Acknowledgements

There are many in her life who filled her with inspiration. The members of the Carrollton Writers Guild (Bob, Eleanor, Richard, Cliff, Gil, Chuck and Cecilia) welcomed, supported, and guided her work.

And her beloved yellow Lab, Tikva, and the two feline nemeses Axel and Karmel, the four-paws who appear in her poetry.

Foreword

Carolyn (known as Cadgie to her family and friends) was my friend for sixty-one years. We were there for each other through childhood, college, marriages, birth of our children, divorces and more. There were arguments and times of distress with one another but the friendship endured. We have co-authored two- and one-half novels together (the third to be completed soon). It was her dream to see her work published and she dragged me along for the ride.

Poetry, though, was the love of her life. She found a community of generous and talented poets in the Carrollton Writers Guild. Her time with them helped her talent blossom. While I nagged her to pull the poems into a volume to publish, she was too busy creating to take the time to accomplish that mundane task.

I have recaptured as many of her poetic works as possible. Some are lost in the vagaries of notebooks, thumb drives and computers long abandoned. The categories are her designations for the collected poems.

As you read her creations, she would want you to practice Selah or the time for contemplation (most often found at the end of a Psalm). She embraced this act with her whole heart and being. Your participation would honor her.

Elyse Wheeler, PhD

Emergent

I do not write into the deep, dark night.
I am an early bard.

Even so, I'm often in need of help in being fully woke.
I mumble and mump most days '
til I've had my second ice tea.

Inspiration does not come so easily these days.
It's more akin to pulling teeth.

But, to have those moments when a line is just right;
That's when it comes into clarity,
My need to write is an act of love, a selfish charity.

Seasons

Winter

Warm blue skies have gone
Shades of green and grey will stay
Cherish those hues left.

Banshee winds howl high
Garage doors are frozen tight
Ice tears freeze on me.

Snow gently falling
Soon it will be appalling
Cold not my calling

Winter Walks

Sliding on wet leaves
Snow slips down my collar
My dog smiles and wags

Snow is falling but the plow has run by.
We have ventured out on this momentary clear path
The flakes fall on my face as the snow keeps falling.
The dog and I trace turkey tracks.
We amble down the street listening for the sound of
       gobbling.

The wind picks up its howling.
Pine trees moan and bend above and the snow keeps
       falling.
I hasten to fasten my coat.
"Humph" the dog grumbles. She thinks I could be more
       organized.
She knows I'll soon be cold
And want to head for home on this beautiful winter's night.

A Snowflakes Journey

I began, surrounded by my brothers and sisters
A warm mist rising from mother ocean.
We rose together. The North wind herding us up, up, up.

We coalesced, rising to new heights.
Daring in our innocent pride
To block the sun from reaching his earthly goal.
As our climb continued,

I realized I was separate.
Alone for the first time. It was cold.
I was cold.
Sharp.

Fragile and fragmented in my own unique way.
Falling, blown and buffeted, travelling fast.
Down ever down until I landed on the ground.

I was next to other members of my family.
I can't wait to go again.

Gifts for the little fletchers

The bird bath is warm.
Water filled.
Titmice drink in swarms.
Chirps and trills

Chill winds toss them high
The feeder is scarred by claws
Wings flap hard
Cling for their life

Cranberries on thread
My Fingers pull
Hopeful gifts of red
To feed my friends and soul

Spring Song

In the Springtime
I hearken back my mind to
The thirsting, thrusting push
Of thistle pulling itself up
Through the winter hard-scrabble layers of marshland and
    rocky ways.

I stand poised:
Watching.
Waiting.
Listening,
For the whistle of the
Meadowlark.
His rapturous song rises
Sparking the air with joyous desire joining the glimmer in
    his eye
Searching for his own true love.
His aria lends itself to all the glamour an avian romance
    will produce.

She moves; a slight thing in the hidden grasses.
Tremulous, twittering she warbles her inquiry
Singing a doubtful descant to his promises of love.

His wings waft with
His rising scent
His romancing but an
Inkling of the summer's coming indolence and passions.
The richness it will surely bring: Nests, Food, and Love
    aplenty

The force of elusive heath and heather's fairy perfume
Fill my heart and mind in my springtime stroll this day.

01/27/67

April Crescendo

This is a silent time
An inhalation of anticipation
Growth requires energy
Buds in trees are swelling and
The grass needs raking.

It's a grown-up game of pick-up sticks.
Cool breezes lighten the work of the day.
Grackles scan the feeder
Seeking the land of plenty for their feathered, hungry horde

The birds get louder
And the grass is greening
Breath gives life a chance for motion
Outdoor living soon

The painted deck is my new room
Family's here with their voices loud as birds.
Gray grass is fading as green rises from her sleep.
Gaia greets her lover sun

Sparrows lilt their tune
Birds are operatic with their blessings
They shower us below with their songs of life and birth.
Passion blazes hot and for the moment,
Questions are silenced by a kiss

Backyard Nocturne

The summer's evening concerts are hushed
Peepers don't shout out their love songs for all to hear.
Crickets lie silent, their legs stiffened:
Their good luck ended by an evening's frost that quietened
    their life's energy.

These early fall evenings recall the moans of wind,
That claim tree branches cracking and then fall in the night.

While the moon waxes, wanes,
Leaves rustle with autumnal urgency.
They fall, deep into the restful earth
Asserting their privilege to nourish
Mother tree one last time.

Rapture of the Season

Mr. Groundhog goes trundling in the median
Cars go speeding as he waddles and he flees again
Colors in the trees they're as pretty as can be
All I can do, all I can think about, is the rapture of the
      season.

Watch the pretty colors brighten and blaze on.
Look up at the birds flying over the pretty autumn haze.
We all need live fully in these joyful golden days.
Yeah. This is what I think about. All that I see is the rapture
      of the season.

I watch fallen leaves rising as creatures scamper through
      them
They are hustling to store food and looking for good
      shelter.
Well, the sun still shines on these busy golden days
And all I dream about, is the rapture of the season
And the joy that precedes our hibernating ways.

Riding through the valley I hear the ghosts all laughing.
They are eating cider doughnuts and maybe contra
      dancing.
Can't you hear the echo of that lively fiddle music?
All I can do, all that I hear is the rapture of the season.

Climbing up the valley - heading west toward sunset
Shadows getting longer - is that Sleepy Hollow's
      horseman?
The pumpkin on the floorboard is acting pretty nervous
All I can do, while I just shake about, is just get shivers in
      this rapturous season!

The wind is singing through the oak and aspen trees
Rollicking the reds and yellows down to find their final
    ease.
Acorns drops their gifts aplenty to the waiting ground
Listen to the earth's good hungry sounds, all the good
    living is the rapture of what's now found.

Apple pies and cinnamon come drifting through the air.
Grey clouds start charging up the steps of the dance
Hear the geese a honkin' sayin' see ya later next year!
And all I can do, all I can taste, all I can dream about is the
    rapture of the Season.

02.01.92

FAMILY

Uppity Children

We are the children of some uppity women.
Some were Signers at Seneca Falls.
We are the children of women who dared to
Make a great difference. They were taught to
Stand up and stand tall.

It will never make sense to sit still and be quiet
When injustice and lies try so hard to rule.
My grandmother's mother was loud and indignant
And her grandchildren's children bred true.

We will march with our brothers and sisters
We will sit in a large city hall
I hope we will urge others to start voting
Watch as we all rise standing tall.

There Will Always Be Loss

She's found walking on that rippled edge,
Balance beamed - a scallop's shell;
That holds her love and keeps exhaustion at bay.
She walking, ponders;
How long can her love continue so muted, care-fully bound
While other's care-less words always hold sway?

The shorelines rise in a quicksilver way.
Waves remind her throat to clench in rhythm.
There will be no speaking of this longing for freedom
Her own anguish.
Yearns for the return to herself
That's been stuck on a shelf.

She bends, wrenching, strains to obtain a release
From these dismal days.
The land keeps on darkening,
The sky holds no blue.

Siblings

(The past)

We are on a Family trip. Dad was the driver.
My baby brother Jon (age two years to my nine years) sat
    in the front center.
He was blanket wrapped in the sixty's version
Of a car seat that hooked over the top.
Mom was to his right.
My brother Chip sat behind Dad and I was behind Mom.
When we weren't punching or pinching each other, we all
    sang Barbershop Quartet songs Dad taught us.

(The Present)

We have a deck that sits two levels high
And it's great to watch all the different birds and creatures.
Especially the half dozen hummingbirds who rise, twitter,
    and strafe each other.
The battle grew heated last night.
One exasperated fledgling flew over and tapped his sister
    on the head.
All we could do was laugh.

Siblings continued

(Past)

As we drove through Illinois, Pennsylvania, and the Finger Lakes in Upstate New York,
We saw beautiful silos and large gatherings of Cows.

"Look Jon," said Chip, "Moo Cows!"

"Bow Wows!!" said Jon.

Chip wasn't having this.
He was the eldest brother and he *knew* he was right.
"MOO Cows!" Chip shouted.

"Bow Wows." Jon muttered

"MOO COWS!" Chip pounded his fist against the door.

Dad said, "Enough!"

Thirty seconds later, Jon muttered, "Bow Wows."
Mom, Dad and I laughed and laughed about it.

Birds in the nest agree?
I say, "BOW WOWS"

Love Began with a Casual Glance.

Love began with a casual glance.
This time, it was found in a cafeteria.
He was smitten.

She was wary.
"I'm sure he's taken, he is so adorable."

"Besides, I don't have time for romance." They both said.

And yet, he persisted.
She resisted for as long as she could.

Joy begets the foundation of a worthy life.
Couplehood grows like a fine oil painting.

And stretches through the framework of thoughtful art and
      creative imaginings
That they are and will be together.

It began with a glance, becoming eternal love.

Hard dreams

Dreams feel more real than the waking world.
I hear mumbled conversations
While walking through the land at my parent's farm.
Their words aren't meant for me.
The sound of their mutual love is wonderful.
I watch seagulls flying overhead.
Each raspberry bush is treasured and tasted.

I wander down to my favorite place,
Passing the Christmas trees that stand as soldiers.
I reach the little pond that has its own island in the middle.
Spring water keeps it fresh.
I gaze at the large scrub pine who is the queen of this small
      domain.

Canada goose families with six or seven goslings tour the
      perimeter.
Sometimes they rest on the island.
Their small peeping noises let all know who is present and
      accounted.

Black eels dwell deep in the pond water.
I first discovered them while wandering with my younger
      brother.
"Let's throw some M-80s in the water. It should make a great
      echo."

The vision of the rising, writhing, bodies killed by our innocent
      play
Shames me to this day.

TAROT

This is a project started in the early 2010s. The goal was a poem for each of the major arcana cards but Death came walking too soon.

The Empress is Having a Bad Day.

I sit on my throne.
Indeed, it is my only home.
My black cat sits upon my lap.
She says since she lies on me, all those who approach are
      truly *her* subjects.

Oh! These subjects of mine!
Fertility demands from the endless twos and threes
Jack endlessly hovering around me, belittling my king and
      asking for...
Well, never mind.
A Royal *must* be discreet.

What would this pack of followers say
If I dared to express my dismay
I don't wish to be a cheerleader
Or light up their room any more in any way.

Let me grouch and drink my tea in silence.
I'd love, for once, not to know before all others.
And quit this job of being the endless mother.

The Hermit

If a mind is a cave, then yes, that's where I live.
Endless pathways lead to
Crystalline thoughts.

The drawings of bears and bison
Reflect the many who batter against me
While I try to finish my thoughts.

I don't hate you.
I just don't need you in my life.
Life is deep and complex demanding the full participation
Of my heart and soul.

Let me be quiet and free
To be ready to guide when the need comes to be.

Death Was Walking

Death was walking
Toward his certain goal
Grumbling to himself
About his heavy load.

Fool came dancing toward him
His was looking at the stars
He didn't see his old friend
As his hands played a guitar.

"Hey! You Fool!
Won't you even say hello?"
But Fool kept right on going
To a pub set right below.

Death began to bellow.
He chased his nutty friend.
Walked right up behind him
And said, "You've a wrong to mend."

"Dear Death, I didn't see you coming!"
Said this merry fellow.
"Come listen to my song
And tell me if it makes you mellow."

Death sighed and grabbed a beer
"You can't take him to task" he said.
I might as well have some joy
Before I find my luckless dead.

He listened to Fool's great rambling song.
It took all afternoon.
Many beers were shared
As he listened to the endless tune.

Death Was Walking continued

"My God, I'm late!" Death cried
As the sun began to sink.
"I need to do my job.
What will the Empress think?"

Fool's grin grew even wider
Than it had been all afternoon.
"She'll know I won the wager—
That I'd keep you from her room."

"You'll have one more year
To think how you will catch her
I'm betting you'll win next time
Or you'll get our nasty emperor.

Animals

Cat Reveries

One

Crushed ice
Causes our small cat great delight.
She does not meow.
She squeaks and trills when she hears the ice machine
    grinding away.
I toss a small chunk out, letting it ricochet against the
    counters.
She runs after it and then lies in wait for the next piece.
Her backside wiggles in anticipation.
She bats her latest victim around like a hockey puck.
We call this game Ice Mice.
Woe until me if I'm thirsty and don't look down to see this
    eager player.

Cat Reveries continued

Two

Before we became a household that had kittens
Now growing into cats,
I used to do crafts.
Felting woolen birds, I hoped to hang from our Christmas
 tree.
I came home one day to find 5 murdered cardinals and
 bluebirds
Lying in a gory woolen mess on my floor.
"See? We took great care to stop these home invaders.
They won't bother you ever again. Do you have any
 more?"

So, I shut those pesky blighters out of my room!
This was no good!
…And then,
They would lie in wait for the sound of an opened door.
Thumpetty, thumpetty, thump
They'd come racing down the hall
Rushing to get inside,
Looking in vain for more woolen birds.
Out they would go!
They would cry outside, imploring me to let them in.

Ah well.
Crafts don't seem that important anymore,
Compared to a winsome purr.

Dr. Schrodinger's Cats

Dr. Schrodinger's wife went mad
You might even say she had a hissy fit.
Her problem was two hissing kits.
They scrambled and yowled
For days upon end
Until the Doc and his missus began to go crazy

Those felines ran in circles and tossed litter.
They left mice at the door.
The birds declared their home
A definite absolute No Flying Zone.

"You've got the big brain, you best start thinking and doing
 and forget all this patting.
Or you can find a new place to snore." she proclaimed.
"I'll end all our troubles!" he chortled.
"I'll just bet!" she said with a shout.
"You were the one who brought home these darn cats.
Figure how to get them out."

So, he built a cat box filled with salmon, scratch posts,
 catnip and sunlight:
Essentials that would fill any cat's heart with great joy.
"I'll show her I know what I'm talking about."
He opened the door to this wondrously built haven
And the cats wandered in.
And it was too quiet…

They both began shaking with guilt and remorse.
"Do you think they are dead?" Mrs. Schrodinger whispered
"Oh no, I'm quite certain that at least one is alive."
But she nagged and he worried and they argued.
This went on for quite a long while.

Dr. Schrodinger's Cats continued

"Dead or alive, we must know the true answer."
I'm not sure, my dear, you know curiosity killed..."
She frowned so deeply at this remark, he said quite
      quickly,
"All right. We'll do it together, on my count of three."
So, they opened the door the poor fellow and woman
And dropped into a wide-open space.

They looked up.
And looked down.

And saw with great horror
Their window diminished
There weren't any doors.
The kitties got out.
Here's how they did it.
They knew
You can't leave Schrodinger's box unless someone is in it.

February 8, 2017

Getting ready to go

Dusk is coming on.
It's warm, almost cozy, like a woman in a ruffled cozy dress
Who's settled in for a comfortable conversation.
We sit on our high deck.
It's that lovely time when the shadows are longer,
The light illuminates the plants and bushes with a deep
    golden glow.

Bees are swarming around one of our nectar feeders.
They dance in a vertically circular rhythm, rising up
Then sinking below the feeder in a curious way.
Hummingbirds chirrup and chireep,
Announcing their presence at the other seven feeders.
They rise, weightless then swoop up and round as flying
    warriors.
Their buzz has a deeper tone than the bees.

A new singer has joined the chorus from the sunroom.
Our longhaired cat posts herself by the window screen
She begins her chortling doing her best to convince the
    tiny birds
To come in ... come in and play inside
Since the Guardians of the deck won't release her.

9/22/20

Pizzicato Paws

Pizzicato paws climb swiftly up cat mountain.

Tail wags from a happy lab add a fine percussive beat.

The rain increases its volume, as it responds
To the symphonic efforts of our beloved musicians.

There is a small pause, and then!
A grand glissando as the cats descend,
Becoming the warm and cozy creatures
Nestled in my friend's lap.

Sneezing

My dog sneezes, her whole body goes into the effort.
Her front paws lift. Her tail moves to increase her balance.

"Achoo!"

Then, she shakes herself to clear the sneeze settings.

Dad used to sneeze so loudly, dust would shake down
    from the rafters.
"Bill!" Mom scolding, as if he could do something to prevent
    that horrifying racket.

She would sneeze so daintily
Dad and I would look around to see where that noise
    occurred.

I often have images of our fluffy cat sneezing.
I picture her body expanding, like a quick blooming
    dandelion then,

Boom!

Of course, she reassembles immediately.
I'm *certain* this occurs.
But she is a stealth sneezer, just like Mom.

Three Donkeys

Down in the meadow where there is a shady tree
Three donkeys stood; Daddy, Mama and baby made three
The parents weren't much for playing
But that baby boy, he just loved to dance
He would gambol and prance and kick up his heels
They would cause me to look every time I'd pass and
I'd smile all the way home.

One day as I drove by
Two stern figures gazed at the small one
His head pressed against the hole where a limb had been
       cut
What had he done to make him so sad or ashamed?
I realized all creatures must have a naughty corner
Even if it's a knotty tree.

Vultures

Vultures have returned to my town.
Not one or two
Or three or five
It's closer to two or three hundred.
Perhaps I exaggerate.
I saw them the other day;
Avian spectrals orbiting
Reminiscent of Van Gogh's circles
A nightmare's starry night.

They were hovering, looming, and lurching
Above the Elementary School.
Last year, I noticed
They liked to perch
On the rooftops of the Middle School.

I've never seen enemy action taken by a single bird.
Maybe they enjoy the cast-offs from lunches.

Because I visit dark places in my mind,
I worry some small child who was
Always left behind
Had been chosen as this year's winter feast.

That small one,
Most careful to be unnoticed
Remains so in our human world
Is now deeply beloved and remembered
By his feathered tribe.

On the passing of her beloved Labrador retriever

Tikva

She's become so thin.
And she is very tired.
Her eyes still brighten when I speak to her.
Then she lies down again.

My gentle friend, I can't bear this.
My quiet one, who always had a comforting presence.
I can't stop weeping.
I will be there for you.

I'll carry you with me when you're gone.

December 2019

APOCRYPHAL

During the Covid Pandemic

A New Kind of Life

To be safe
To be protected
I must rise with the birds to extend my life.
The birds sing.

Within the confines of my car
As I travel to the bank
And the grocery store
I sing too.

The authorities on Facebook
Say the singing spreads the virus.
But in my car -
Alone
I sing with the birds.

Pandemic in Three Parts

Pandemic Part One

The world stalker
Glides
Mindlessly slinking in its eerie path
To its newest victim.

She gasps. Then coughs while fear
Fills her lungs and heart.
"I will not let this affect me."
She says to herself.
"There are too many people who need me.
I'm too busy to get sick. "

Every death begins in denial.
The bodies mount up.
The caregivers refuse to give up.
The body count of the innocent keeps growing.

Pandemic Part Two

The Bloody Politicians search for someone to blame
For their indifference and greed.
They hope their enemies will be the ones to die.
The mindless followers move like angry Zombies
Shouting out nonsense they fervently believe in.
"Covid's a lie.
They just want to control us.
Fox News tells us different"
The people in charge laugh and urge their believers toward
    greater conflict
The center fails. More people are dying.
The leaders long for the time of the crematoriums.
The elders are quiet. They know they'll be next on the list
    of the targeted villains
The leaders whisper to each other "Let's just expose them
    so they'll die. Then the scare will be over."
"We won't have so many to care for. This is working well in
    the nursing homes."
"Mass graves will be the answer. Then there won't be such
    a high body count."

Pandemic Part Three

They tell us our unemployment Figures are at 14%
But those who are on furlough are not factored in.
The true unemployed is at 25%
We all know things are worse.
They tell us Listen only to the leader who lies the minute
    he begins to speak
We wonder who has the talking heads so frightened they
    cannot tell the truth?
We all know things are worse.
We all know things are going to get worse.

This poem was published in West Georgia Woman

Searching for an Alleluia.

We are wandering slowly
Feeling depressed, lost, and lonely.
Distracted by the worry that seems to hold dominion
While our shadow selves grow in power with their
Formidable opinions.

We are not truly socially distant
To keep our faith, to be persistent in love
I swear to you; patience, kindness, and caring
Are the first gifts to be sharing.

We can beat this virus with our love.

Black Horse Riding

I've been riding on the black horse
Wanting you to understand
Armageddon comes to every life and
Despair thrives with in each man.

Hangmen know me.
Judge and juries
Sometimes see me
In a fleeting vision -
When they hear how hard the victims cried.
They think they see me slowly trotting by, asking;
"Are you as innocent as that long-gone soul?
Can you be as guilty as the one you try?"

My black horse runs as time gets closer
For me to meet my brothers
And do some feasting in the time nearby.

We have always been here.
We are the secret Armageddon. We came a dawning in Gethsemane
Our derisive laughter came rising even louder
When we heard Peter's lamentations over the morning's
      rooster crows.

Black Horse Riding continued

We've been getting ready for our final time by:
Crusading with the shining children.
Fiestas at the Inquisition.
Dancing through the Black Plague,
We four standing rosy in the Ring.
We danced mad polkas shoeless in the crematoriums
Where our hunger for the flames grew in exponential ways.
Maxing out our harsh rejoicing when we saw two towers
      fall.

I am riding on my black horse
Hoping soon you'll understand.
Armageddon's part of every soul
I soon plan to rule this land.

December 24, 2009

America Casts Its Vote. A Prophesy.

We wear the pallor of the shallow
In the cool shadow of our Country's Parlor.
As we gather drinking tea and sherry in our smug
        insolence.
We avoid even thoughts of the squalor the unfortunates
        have endured.

We say,
"Well. They must have brought it upon themselves.
They just weren't *living* right."

Within the time it takes
To bite the cookie,
Sip the tea,
Write a check from our miser's portion
We try to magnify for all to see:

Our Judgment will soar downward.
Our healthy gleaming eyes will refuse to see this sight.

Dark gazes will be cast upon our cataracted souls that will
        start to shriek
As blighted Overseers begin to exact their full judgments
They shall whirl their dervished anger for our Mission's
        weak delivery.

America Casts Its Vote. A Prophesy continued

We shall be the ones dying on the docks.
Lag our step upon the streets, looking for mercy,
Now so willing to eat the black crow's humble pie
As we beg them to forget the many times we could have
    lent a hand.

As we gaze into the starry night, Van Gogh's choice will
    seem so clear.
Anything to stop the sound of the raucous mocking of
    gallows' laughter
Echoing in our goose stuffed souls
As we stagger, slip and crawl toward the edifice
We wrecked in our ego and neglect.

Oct 7, 2011

Righteous Ones

Righteous ones who are up so high
See us wave to you in your heavenly sky.
In your place with God's great plan
Would you dare to grasp our hands?
Mankind's daring, great and strong
I think that grace would have us all belong.

Temptation Ayes

Forty days of fasting
And three times you said no.
Well, *we* could do that.
We can resist that evil doer, we mumble.
You know, you've taught us so.

But every day's a new day
In this desert of wills to survive
Our desire for power
And dreams of glory
To keep a memory of who we've been alive.

We are hard pressed
To stay relentless
Against the oppressor who hisses in our inner ear, "Why?
You deserve to be...
Envious
Angry
Begrudging
Rage against the traffic
Blame the machine of the
Corporation
Union
Republicrat
And by all means forget that silly notion of forgiveness
      seven times seventy.

The Lenten times burn a blister of desire-
For the easy transformations-
Some effortless solutions in these quick trigger days.
The rigor of putting prayers as actions takes:
Energy.
Love.
And courage.
Three ways to say *yes* in the way you taught us so.

HAIKU

Haiku

Carolyn began writing Haiku with the goal of one every Tuesday for a year. Though maybe not every Tuesday, she far exceeded a year's worth and then some. Dates are provided where known.

Banshee winds howl high
Garage doors are frozen tight
Ice tears freeze on me

Snow gently falling
Soon it will be appalling
Cold—not my calling

On this Fat Tuesday
I think about Lenten fasts
Satisfy by praise

The rain falls so hard
It sounds as I am immersed
My cares downstream, Lord

Worn out and weary.
Feeling almost as dreary
As this dark and rainy day.

Stories travel on
Intertwining lives and songs
Praise of Sorrows Road

Sliding on wet leaves
Rain slipping down my collar
Dog smiles and wags

Buds in trees swelling
Grass needs raking pick-up sticks
Cool breezes lighten

Outdoor living soon
Painted deck is my new room
Voices loud as birds

Grackles scan the feeder
Seeking the land of plenty
Feathered hungry horde

Considering that we are anticipating fallout from a tropical storm and my dear ones have endured a cyclone bomb in New England, here's a seasonal haiku to lead the way into Autumn:

Haiku Bluesday:

I gaze through windows,
Magnolia blossoms bud.
Life's low ebb is gone.

Pink blossoms today.
Weeping cherry, magnolia.
Champions of Spring

Birds operatic
Blessings shower us below
Songs of life and birth

You have slept too long!
Bouncing cat meows exclaims
I have hunger pangs!

Scry the future face
Move forward thoughtful places
Read no whines no blues....

Chlora fills my greens
Dandy lions grace my plains
Verdant life striving

Skunk cabbage rises
Steaming tendrils push on snow
Breaking winter's back
10-13-2019

A tanka is like a haiku, except it has 5-7-5-7-7. That being said, I submit the following for your amusement:

Snow storm of the year
Get your milk and cookies here
It might get scary
So, beware stay tuned listen
We'll let you know when it's clear
01-26-2015

Bright blue summer day
Grass is green. Life's serene
A grumble is futile
06-17-2014

My friend's tiny cat
Stalks and fusses, leaps and hisses
Then she'll cuddle, purr
06-04-2014

Red geraniums
Swinging in their hanging pots
Whippoorwills chant low
05-13-2014

Warm blue skies have gone
Shades of green and grey will stay
Cherish those hues left
11-25-2013

Ode to the Yellow Labrador:

A foghorn hums, I think.
The evening sky is clear?
LABS! Rhythmic snorers!
09-06-2013

Cool day; bright blue skies
Young hawks above learn to fly
I just smile all day
08-06-13

Weatherman's musical prophecy:

We see bands of rain.
Dance in precipitations.
Drum in thunderin'.
05-22-2012

Kidney stone passing
The world is pain forever
Teeth and eyes clench hard
01-17-2012

Snoozy Haiku for you:

Tap on my keyboard
The dog snores low in rhythm
Time to move this day
01-13-2012

Wise men journey on:

Holiday Spirit
We Search for the sacred star
Life's true song uplifts.
12-20-2011

Cranberries streaming!
Bogs harvesting crimson joy.
Tart Yankee pleasure
11-15-2011

Wind sprites sprint by me
Scatter leaves yellow, green, brown
Exuberant Fall
10-25-2011

Drab autumn leaves
Fall to the ground, nonchalant
Sunrise songs low key
10-18-2011

From Kindergarten to PhD Haiku for you:

Let us praise teachers
Passion, Joy, creative ways
Inspire always
08-23-2011

Flocked busy sparrows
Gather seeds and vanish fast
Hidden in holly
08-16-2011

Judas tree sighting
Yellow, red mixed with green leaves
Summer's first farewell
08-09-2011

Dark clouds animate
Sledding children move so fast
Summer's fleeting tale
08-01-2011

The dog split the sky
With sharp barked thunder paws
Blessed canine love
07-19-2011

Cool summer morning
Sunlight plays through shadowed trees
Savor the moment
07-06-2011

Intemperate words
Ona summer's day
Howl frigid warnings
07-01-2011

Farmer's Market start!
Flowers, fruits, distillate goods
Neighbors create joy.
06-28-2011

Long Shadowed Sunsets
The Atlantic's briny scent
Summer by the sea
06-21-2011

Mourning dove grey skies
Good bye and so long bye bye
Changing times are drear
06-14-2011

Sweep up maple seeds!
Wipe off pollen's gift on sills
Think of Winter's salt
06-07-2011

Alpine strawberries
Small ruby sparkle of Spring
Tastes of garden joy
05-24-2011

Swamp maple leaves reach
Implores: Water, warmth and light
Lush supplication
05-10-2011

Magnolia cups.
White or Pink? Green willow straws.
Springtime Tea Party.
05-03-2011

Thor Haiku for you on Tuesday:

Lightning's roving search
Fearsome teeth sink in windows
Pane and trembling shock
04-12-2011

Ice Economics
Snow showers bring more plowers
Budget's slippery slope
02-01-2011

Mid winter's day dream
Warm Bermuda's teal sea scene
Cold gray sings the blues
01-25-2011

Biting, bitter cold
Aching squeak from snow's protest
Tears crack out my eyes
01-24-2011

Pearlescent skies crowd
Treed ravines keen for deep snow
Silent expectation
01-11-2011

There are times in life
When sunlight's overbearing
January glare
01-04-2011

Ivy wrapped on pines
As tight a coat could be
Nature's Christmas tree
12-21-2010

Barometric Haiku for you:

Water colored blue
Encaged in glass it seems til
Pressure spills it out
12-14-2010

Grey Hooded Figure
Walks on Desolation Road
Where the Angels sing?
12-07-2010

Tuesday Thankful Haiku:

"Celia's service dog's name is Tikva. It means Hope in Hebrew. Simcha is the Hebrew word for great joy and gladness. Tikva has given our daughter and our family great joy, gladness and healing with her presence. Samcha is the word for celebration and Tikva greets us all with her loving spirit every time we reenter her space." CLH

Tikva. Service dog
Samach. Great joy and gladness
Simcha. Welcome home
11-23-2010

Brothers. Sister, Me
Children's traits true and straight
Music, Spirit. Love
10-26-2010

Transit green to gold
Summer's lushness. Autumn's bold
New world unfolding
10-17-2010

Tuesday's EEEUW Haiku:

Colonoscopy.
Tomorrow. Not good today.
Sunny side up soon
10-5-2010

Tuesdays Achoo Haiku:

Scratchy throat sore eyes.
Tomato juice please save me.
Help me start my day!
09-28-2010

Fall's a bluegrass tune
Feathered hearts hear a southern song
Leaves change two-step time
09-21-2010

My shaky arms stretch
embrace my sturdy tabletop
glad for its strong legs
09-07-2010

A car's siren calls
Dogs are barking in the air?
Mockingbird! Mocks me.
09-07-2010

September Light blows
A different blue; cool, sleek
Yielding to dark soon.
09-06-2010

Haiku for Idealist.org

Endless need inspires
Energy. Devotion. Love.
Ideals in motion
08-24-2010

The Media thinks:
You are so mindless. Wrong Fox.
No Palindrome Me
08-24-2010

Willow branches stretch
Springing twists- a dryad's tree
Wraiths weep grimace flee
08-17-2010

Tomato season!
Bright red glory summers song.
Concentrated joy.
08-10-2010

Duel! Young Hawk Intrudes.
Arrows flight Winged sparrow.
Kree! Hawk says. I flee
08-03-2010

Living flotsam flows.
Love arrives, has tea and goes.
Leaves to read alone.
07-27-2010

Tidal erasure.
Walks on sand and rocky ways.
Friendship's fleeting smile.
07-20-2010

Lawns are faded brown
Lilies bloom roses decline
July is August now.
07-14-2010

Heat humidity.
Humbling fluidity.
Salt etched on my face.
07-06-2010

Morning's dew shimmers.
Summer's joy rises early.
Salt air wafts to me.
06-22-2010

Women meet at night
Caring smiles fearless sharing
Mercy in action!
06-15-2010

Mom's black satin clutch.
Hanky clenched, scented, lipsticked.
Risen past comes greeting.
06-10-2010

Rugosa is red
And my lavender is blue
Trend scenting walkways
05-18-2010

Tuesday Brain Eating Haiku:

Right Red Coral Bells
Suck flies in their ghastly stalks
Petite zombie treats
04-27-2010

My doorway has a special guest
A mother robin's built her nest
Hiding in the holly tree
Red breasted armor protects her blue-shelled three.
04-20-2010

Birds' songs lift upward
Trees and grass add a descant
Springs joyful concert.
04-13-2010

The rains are streaming
Rivers are rising so high
I see water views!
03-30-2010

Young woman hopping
Showered clean runs fast hugging
Smiles brighter than rain
03-23-2010

I am thinking: fly!
Gorgeous. Soaring. Lift up High
Spirit breathing free
03-16-2010

Skunk cabbage rises
Streamed tendrils lead to the
Winters broken back
03-09-2010

Stretching out the spine
Neck squeals kinda feels like heck
Yoga? Barely. Boo.
03-01-2010

Heavy frozen rain
Cracking colors slash my panes
Winter window blues
02-23-2010

TRANSITIONS

Transitions

Skunk cabbage rises
Steaming tendrils push on snow
Breaking winter's back

Bright blue summer day
Grass is green Life's serene
A grumble is futile

Judas tree sighting
Yellow, red mixed with green leaves
Summer's first farewell

Fall's a bluegrass tune
Feathered hearts hear a southern song
Leaves change two-step time

Biting, bitter cold
aching squeak from snows protest
tears crack out my eyes

Top of the world

We began in Mother Ocean.
Her salinity honored by our very Life's Blood.
Instead of floating in her, womb-like,
We became restless, following the moons tidal pull.
We saw dryness.
The amazing Brown Blue and the green.
Our eyes gave us the will to grow arms and moving appendages until finally,
We crawled upon the land.
Forgetting her, we forged our own new worlds.
Until my brother and I realized we missed our home.
We began our long journey home until the final day
When we stood in exultation before her,
She murmured sadly on the shore "You can visit, but you can't ever come home."

Psychopomps

Berkeley's Polyphore
surrounds the tree at the lowest trunk line
embracing it as pantaloons hugged young French
        maidens.
This Saprotrophic Fungi
Blooms new layers every year

As the tree enters its death cycle
The cellulose layers are transformed
Endocytosis creating this step, a passage down the river
As a source for a new kind of life for the dead.

Ma Joad's American Song

She stands there eager to shield them from the pain of
    their doubting times;
The particular striving that forms a family ideal.
Ma's at the root of it all, hearing the call, finding their worth
searching for value, digging the gold away from our dearth
    and she sings:

"And oh, I'll hold a candle firmly for you standing strong
    against the dark.
Oh, and I will love you strong and remind you of this word
    called hope.
Yes, dear, hope's the only thing they cannot tear straight
    from your soul.
They will try to take it right alive but do not let it go.
I say, never let that go.
This candle will sputter.
Spill wax into the gutter, but I will never let my love for you
    be denied."

The wind bends her back, blowing hard, wet and cold; she stands there strong holding on to her goals. The chill stars, they call out to her; remain as yourself and stand proud rise tall in your soul. How do I guide them to walk from the reins of desire, their wish to reach high above poverty's mire.

Ma Joad's American Song continued

"And oh, I'll hold a candle for you standing strong against
      the dark.
Oh, and I will love you strong and remind you of this word
      called hope.
Yes, dear, hope's the only thing they cannot tear straight
      from your soul.
They will try to take it right alive but do not let it go.
I say, never let that go.
This candle will sputter.
Spill wax into the gutter, but I will never let my love for you
      be denied."

October 26, 2009

My Home Town

The Atlantic dwells at the end of my town
Five miles of beach land protect the bay
Gulls are there and Sandpipers abound.

A Pilgrim's Monument is astride a hill you have to climb a ways
Winding paths ever steeper lead you to the top of the world
You can see hundreds of miles of seashores and sand if skies aren't cloudy and gray

The harbor was deep enough for Clipper Ships, built with sails unfurled
Launched upon the ocean, with Sailors, cordage, tar and pine
Captains and crews came back to their homes with a narrow vision uncurled

The moon pushes seawater in, bringing the scent of unique Atlantic brine
A new story happens as tidal waters come in making a lovely sound
And an old story continues as the waters go out, teaching us all about time.

12 Lines
Tarza Rima
Rhyme scheme aba bcb cdc dad

Time travel through touch

Nothing feels so lush
As grass between my toes
sense rejuvenates my aching bones.
I'm thrown way back to being the kid
who travelled down ravines
seeking danger and imaginary troubles
within my wildest dreams.

Calling out to my good friends
"Can you come and play today
it's a fine, fine time to be pirating
or to be dark spies today.
let's go climb on our bicycles
they'll be our faithful steeds or
to be Robin Hood
will be incredibly good
on these days of make believe.

I think these days are over
then I glance up at my screen
laughing at myself
for believing I'm all grown up
when I walk for miles
in my imagination and
now I get to write it down.

2020

Prufrock's Niece

The grocery is crowded. I bumble my way around crowds.
Anxiety mounts as I search for the perfect products.
Three stores later, I have my list completed.

Before I begin cooking, there are floors to vacuum, areas
    that need tidying.
"You don't need to clean for me. I haven't come to visit
    your house."
Rings a false reassurance.

Four hours later, the house is as spotless as I can make it.
The meal is ready except for the final flourishes.
Low flowers are carefully placed on the set table.

A clean apron protects my unspotted shirt.
My skirt is long, my feet, bare and comfortable.
A tremulous smile masks my anxiety as I open the door for
    my beloved
And joy heals my shattered nerves.

Out of time

Growing up in the time of Twiggy
with my Rubenesque body
required endless attempts to fit in.

Field hockey and athletics were the stars
That shined in the Bully girls' eyes in high school.
They wore their stick straight hair in pigtails
my uncontrolled curls were cut short
(mother's edict 'my house, my rules").

Mockery and rape were on the bullies' mind
Inviting me over so the older brother of one of the team
      came in and tried to force me.
I broke away and ran with my clumsy steps all the way
      home.

Music had always called to me
My church singing friends said I was too blunt.
I wasn't welcome.

Retreating, I found comfort in the library,
reading psych cases to understand
How the mind can cope with different casualties.

05/31/2020

SONGS

Part of these lyrics appear in Raven's Eye, the first volume of the Foxhaven Trilogy

Straight to You

It's been a rock-hard uphill journey
with no hope nor sanctuary given
and though the tracks I've beaten here have long been
      solitary
I knew well my rhythms I knew well my drumming beat.

I can't help but be amazed
Finding my joy is mirrored in you
I'm the one who sees the darkling moons
But now I'm asked to join your luminescent dance.

(Refrain)
When I feel this exultation
Instead of dire lamentations
This sense of warmth and healing
That brings me straight to you
The meteor comes shining
Reflects the sun's great glory
Can it be that loves real story
Isn't ridicule and lies?

Straight to You continued

Can I quit this long preoccupation
To stop the dragon's roar
Thwart the grey eyed jabber sworn to make me stagger,
    watch me fall
When now I see a rainbow color rising on my onyx walls.
I cannot keep a sense of balance when I see your shining
    eyes
I hear the answer of those colors when your heart beats
    next to mine
I've found joy I never dreamed of in my deepest yearning
The sense that you have looked for me as well.

Out here in the orbit of transplanetary solitude
I understood the magnitude of facing life alone
I wandered ever lonely, always searching for my only
Then you came and brought me home, then you came and
    brought me home

(Refrain)
When I feel this exultation
Instead of dire lamentation
This sense of warmth and healing
That brings me straight to you
The meteor comes shining
Reflects the sun's great glory
Can it be that loves real story
Won't be ridicule and lies?

Here's a fun little lyric I hope will appear in the second book of Foxhaven Chronicles

A riff by Chad and Scotty
Beat set to the rhythm of Take Five

A Little Night Music

Last night
Almost sleeping
I heard
Rhythm
In the beauty of the night.
Stars were dancing
Their Light just blazing
Night birds singing
Tales of wonder and romance.

They sang
"Join in,
Join us
Join the chorus
You know it's
Time for a little
Frolic
Let's have a good fling
Into life and all its delights
So, won't you join us?
Join the chorus
We will drink up starlight and romance.
Join us!
Join the chorus.
Kick your heels, give joy a chance."

John B. MacIntyre (Mac) grew up in New Orleans. A scene in Raven's Eye inspired this comedic romp.

Some Zombies still have ears....

Broken Backs
Screaming Cats
Un-life gets in the way
I'm not having so much fun
With zombies climbing
From the bay

If we get a good run going
As we leave the cemetery
Well, then I'll stop and ask you why
My life goes on this way.
I meant no disrespect when I said to you in passing
"Zombies minds are just decayed.
All zombies could be beaten.
We could out run them
Before we got gnawed on."
What in the world do you think got them so mad
There's talk of a filet of <u>me</u> on
<u>Zombie Food</u> tonight?

Chorus
Oh! Broken backs
and Screaming cats
Un life gets in the way
I'm not having so much fun
With zombies walking
Toward me and talking Étouffée

Some Zombies still have ears....continued

Well, we've left the graveyard far behind us
But I hear them mumbling now
"I'll take the tall one's shank
And you can have his upper brow"
I'm not looking to be a zombie po'boy
And I know you don't wanna be a man wich
We need to find a way to find the queen who will
Do what she do to voo doo
Us out of this very bad how you do do.

Chorus

Broken backs
screaming cats
Un-life gets in the way
I'm not having so much fun
with zombies walking
toward us their lips dropping on the way.

Finally, the song that resonated in her heart. She sang the words many times and despite her efforts, she never learned to read music. The tune is lost.

Selah

Selah. Selah
Find your meaning with me.
Selah. Selah
Stop. Look. See the Beauty of my world.

Selah.
Listen well.
Prepare yourself for your time with me.

Learn to yield so you can endure
Humility can be a joyful cure
Selah, take a breath with me
Selah and remember me.

Selah Selah
This is your time to pause
Selah Selah
Rest for a holy time with me

Selah go beyond amen
Beyond our sacred time together again
Stop. And remember quite well
That the Selah will travel with you if you will only Look.
I know you will realize when you see
You are the beauty of my world to me.
Selah. My most sacred time. Selah.
Remember you're mine

October 18, 2009

Carolyn's Bio in her own words.

I admit it. I am a spiritual child of Walter Mitty, James Thurber's character who lived his real life in stories he made up while coping with his every day, humdrum life.

I loved to pretend. I still do. Writing about time travel, being a musician, a goofy (but brilliant) member of the English elite is a wonderful way to spend my time. I hope you'll also find a fine escape as well in the Fox Haven and Waterton series.

When I'm not wandering around in alternate universes, I'm the proud mother of Celia Ann. She looks at the world in quite unusual ways. My children's book, *Celia and The Land of Discouraging Words* is the result of an evening's conversation. The town I lived in for many years provided love and support when one of my family members was seriously hurt. *I love Summer the Best* is my love letter to the town that was more than willing to help.

Music provides the heartbeat in my life. You'll find lyrics that reflect Charlie's love for Sami, and Mac's worries about zombies. You just never know who will have a lyrical story to tell.

My writing partner and lifelong friend, Elyse Wheeler, has helped me to grow in many ways. It's so wonderful to think about the following questions: What am I seeing, tasting, smelling, touching and hearing? She reminds me that the world doesn't always center around dialogue. I'm grateful to have her constancy and brilliance in my life.

The Carrollton Writers Guild has provided wonderful support for my story telling and poetry. I urge you to find a group that will help you to refine your stories.

www.ingramcontent.com/pod-product-compliance
Lightning Source LLC
Chambersburg PA
CBHW030159100526
44592CB00009B/360